Ramblings
RANDOM RECOLLECTIONS

William C. Potter

©2024 All rights reserved.

Independently published
William C. Potter
Melbourne, Florida, U.S.A.

ISBNs
979-8-9889048-3-0 – Softcover
979-8-9889048-4-7 – Epub

TABLE OF CONTENTS

Foreword 4
Bosnia and Herzegovina 5
Sarajevo 18
Commencement Address 26
An Afternoon with the Kid 31
The Journey of *Island Girl* 42
Business Hall of Fame Acceptance Speech 58
Acknowledgments 63
Bibliography 65
About the Author 66

Foreword

I practiced law in Brevard County, Florida, for more than 35 years. Although the practice of law includes some exciting experiences, most of the practice consists of going to the office every day and dealing with rather mundane matters. I have, however, had a few experiences which stand out for me and are different than those experienced by most small-town lawyers.

I wrote about one of those unusual experiences in my book *A Bosnian Diary: A Floridian's Experience in Nation-Building*, published by the Florida Historical Society in 2006. That book described what was undoubtedly the most exciting and challenging professional experience of my career. I have, however, included in this book some of the experiences in Bosnia and Herzegovina which I did not relate in that earlier book.

The recollections in this book also describe a couple of other experiences which are memorable to me. One experience was my meeting with my childhood hero Ted Williams. The other was our sail across the Atlantic in a 44-foot catamaran. Although I realize that these recollections will be of very limited general interest, I am hopeful that they might strike a chord with a few people who can relate to my enthusiasm for these experiences.

I included the commencement address at Holy Trinity and the Business Hall of Fame acceptance in this book even though they were not "adventures" in the same sense as the other stories. However, I ran across them when putting this book together and was a bit surprised that some of the thoughts expressed seem to remain relevant several years after I expressed them, so decided to include them.

Bill Potter

Bosnia and Herzegovina

In 1997, I had an opportunity with the Air National Guard which would literally change my life. I had been promoted to the grade of Colonel in 1991. The Air Force required that lawyers who attained that grade be trained for an additional war-time mission. The reasoning was that if a JAG Colonel is called to active duty, he/she will likely outrank the active-duty JAG, a result that the Air Force did not like. Therefore, JAG's who were promoted to the grade of Colonel had to be qualified as Civil Affairs Officers as well as JAG's. In the Air Force, a Civil Affairs Officer is basically an advisor to a foreign government. In order to be so qualified, I took the Army Civil Affairs Officer Course conducted by the Special Warfare School at Fort Bragg, NC. Thus, when the Air National Guard began looking for officers to send to war-torn Bosnia and Herzegovina (BiH) in 1997, I was among the first to go. My first experience occurred in the fall of that year when I was assigned as an international election supervisor for the first election in BiH since the war ended in November 1995. Although the war had ended almost 2 years before, there remained sporadic fighting around the country and tensions were high. I flew to Zagreb, Croatia, where we underwent training in preparation for conducting the elections. The Dayton Peace Agreement which ended the war gave responsibility for elections to the Organization for Security and Cooperation in Europe (OSCE) which I quickly learned to describe as the Organization for Spreading Chaos In Europe. After about a week training in Zagreb, I travelled with about 30 other election supervisors to Banja Luka, the capitol of the Republika Srpska (RS), the Serbian entity which comprised half of BiH. I vividly remember the bus ride from Zagreb to Banja Luka and the utter and complete destruction that began about 40 kilometers before the border with BiH and continued all of the way to Banja Luka. We drove through towns where there was literally not a single building which had not been destroyed. We drove through forests in which all of the trees had been felled by artillery fire. When we arrived in Banja Luka, we found that it had not been devastated as badly as the rest of the RS and there were some intact buildings. The most noticeable damage in Banja Luka were the mosques which had all been completely destroyed and even the rubble had been hauled off lest the Muslims return and try to rebuild their places of worship. Banja Luka was the center of the hard-core fanatics who were largely responsible for beginning the war and for ethnically cleansing the predominantly Serb areas of BiH. Many of the people were not particularly friendly to Americans because it was U.S. intervention which had ultimately stopped the war by taking air action against the Serbs. Although I was cautioned not to tell people that I was an American, I did not

Author Bill Potter | Photo by unnamed Turkish Soldier

disguise it and was generally treated with friendliness. In Banja Luka, I stayed in a private home with 2 other international election supervisors, and the homeowner was very gracious, even insisting that I join him in drinking some Slivovitz, the fruit brandy that all Bosnians seem to brew in their basements. At that time, there were about 65,000 peace-keeping troops in BiH, about 23,000 of whom were Americans. The peace-keeping force, known as the Stabilization Force (SFOR), was commanded by an American general and included troops from all NATO nations as well as many former Soviet-bloc countries, including Russia and Ukraine. The Banja Luka area was under the jurisdiction of the British Army. While the war was going on, the Brits were really the only troops on the ground who had taken on the Serbs and whipped them badly so the people in Banja Luka were careful not to run amiss of the Brits. There were troops and armored personnel carriers and tanks in evidence throughout the RS. The British soldiers in Banja Luka made it clear that they were eager to find an excuse to exact even more pain on the Serbs. After a few days of further training and orientation in Banja Luka, I accompanied 2 other elections supervisors and 2 interpreters to Kotor Varos, a town about 40 kilometers south of Banja Luka, where we were to be the regional supervisors for about 20 voting precincts. This was an interesting assignment because Kotor Varos was perhaps the hardest-core area of Serb nationalism in BiH and had been the scene of some of the most vicious genocide and ethnic cleansing during the war. Our quarters there were in the only hotel in town which was notable for the large hole, about 4 feet in diameter, over the main door which had resulted from a mortar shell fired at the hotel. Kotor Varos was also reputed to be a hiding place for Radovan Karadzic, the former president of the Serb entity during the war who had been indicted for war crimes and genocide by the war crimes tribunal in The Hague. Although SFOR had thousands of troops looking for him, he would avoid capture for another 10 years. In Kotor Varos, there were signs of support for Karadzic all over town and at all of the polling stations. We would pull the posters down but they would quickly be replaced. Kotor Varos was patrolled by Dutch troops who were everywhere. They were notably unfriendly, even to the international election supervisors, and I wondered if their unfriendliness had anything to do with the general disdain of the Dutch that had resulted from the fact that the Dutch had not prevented the Serbs from murdering thousands of Muslim men and boys at Srebenica in July, 1995. Part of our election supervisor contingency in Kotor Varos were 3 members of the Polish Navy with whom I soon developed a friendship. They were all funny and fun-loving. One night, I went to dinner with the 3 Poles and was amused when they began the dinner by offering a toast to the Russian Navy by raising their glasses and proclaiming "Bottoms Up." I had underestimated their hatred for Russians. The elections took place over 2 days of the weekend. We were the regional supervisors so our job was to periodically visit all of the polling stations which were spread over an area within a radius of perhaps 60 kilometers. One particularly poignant moment was when I observed an elderly woman screaming at one of the poll workers. When I inquired about her problem, I was told that she was upset because, never having previously voted in a free election, the poll workers would not tell her for whom to vote. That night, we collected all of the ballot boxes from all of the polling sites and locked them in a room at the city hall in Kotor Varos. However, when we were informed that some of the local politicians were trying to enter the room, we transferred the boxes to our hotel room. We had 2 German policemen, members of the International Police Task Force (IPTF), an agency of the United Nations, who were assigned to provide security for us. When we had some people knocking on our door demanding access to the ballot boxes, the 2 Germans helped us discourage our visitors. In the end, I think that we were confident that we had overseen a clean and uncompromised election. Unfortunately, the ethnic and religious differences were so acute and the fears and hatreds so prevalent that only the radically nationalistic parties could prevail and the elections only accentuated the divisions within the society. For me, the results reinforced my belief that holding elections soon after a bitter civil war only deepens the divisions within a society. The U.S. has repeated that mistake several times since BiH but seems determined to show that elections are the first step to democracy, a thesis which has been consistently disproved.

I was given several false alarms by the Air Force regarding being deployed to BiH. On several occasions, I was verbally informed that the Air Force was going to activate me and deploy me to Sarajevo as a legal advisor. My daughter Alison and her fiance Scott even rescheduled their wedding at least once in contemplation of my leaving. However, as the predicted deployment date approached, there always seemed to be an unexpected change of events. Not until 1999 would I actually receive real orders deploying me to Sarajevo as part of SFOR.

My next assignment as an election supervisor took place in 1998 when I returned to BiH. This time, my assignment was in the Muslim-Croat entity within BiH known as the Federation of Bosnia and Herzegovina (FBiH). Again, I first went to Zagreb, Croatia, where we trained at the

Intercontinental Hotel. Zagreb is a nice city with decent restaurants, some sights to see and generally friendly people. Those who had been to Zagreb prior to the dissolution of Yugoslavia found Zagreb to have changed from a drab socialist city to a vibrant, modern, western-like city. I was struck by the remarkable beauty of the women everywhere we went. From Zagreb, we went by bus to Tuzla, a predominately Muslim city in FBiH. Tuzla, like almost every city in FBiH, had been the scene of heavy fighting and suffering during the war. We were quartered at the Hotel Tuzla. It was there that I met my interpreter who was to become a great friend for life. Amina Bilajic was a 19 years-old young woman who had just completed high school. Amina lived in Gradacac, a small town about 35 kilometers from Tuzla. She had spent about 3 years of her teens living in the basement of her house with no electricity or running water while her town was bombarded every day by the Serb artillery which surrounded the town. Amina was not initially assigned to be my interpreter but when one of the other interpreters asked her to trade so that she could be assigned to a younger man, Amina agreed to work with the old man. For the next couple of weeks, Amina and I worked closely together, first as we prepared for the elections in Tuzla and then in Gradacac as we supervised the election in the town. By the end of the assignment, I had been extremely impressed by Amina's intelligence, poise and kindness. Everywhere we went in Gradacac, everyone knew and admired Amina. When it was time for me to return to Zagreb, I asked Amina if she was interested in coming to the U.S. for college if I could arrange it. She replied that she had a great interest in doing so.

I called Wendy from BiH to ask her whether she would be willing to try to bring Amina to the U.S. and have her attend college while living with us. Wendy's only question was whether Amina smoked cigarettes which I assured her she did not. We later checked with the rest of the family who all enthusiastically supported bringing Amina to live with us. I found that, in order to obtain a student visa for Amina, I would have to obtain an admission certificate from a college and also show financial support for her that would be sufficient to ensure that she would not require public assistance. I was able to convince the local community college to issue an admission certificate even though her high school transcripts were unavailable due to the fact that it had been completely destroyed during the war. Moreover, the Test of Foreign Language (TOFL), normally required for admission of foreign students, was not available in BiH. Thus, although they issued an admission certificate, they made it clear that they would allow her to take only English as a Second Language (ESL). I was okay with that restriction because I was confident that we could deal with that after she was here. I called Amina to tell her that I would be sending the Admission Certificate together with a financial affidavit listing our assets and agreeing to be financially responsible for her. The first time I called was kind of awkward because her brother answered the phone and spoke not a word of English. After I floundered around for a few sentences, he understood that I was speaking English and called Amina to the phone. While I was speaking to Amina, I could hear her father in the background asking the kind of questions that any loving father would have about his daughter speaking with an unknown man 6,000 miles away seeking to convince his daughter to leave home. It is a real tribute to the love of her parents and their confidence in her good judgment that they allowed her to come to the U.S. With the Admission Certificate and my financial information in hand, Amina and her father were able to travel to the U.S. embassy in Zagreb and obtain a student visa. I sent her a plane ticket and in early January, 1999, Amina arrived in the U.S. That was kind of an adventure because her plane first took her to Atlanta where she would go through customs and change flights for Melbourne. In order to assist her in navigating the Atlanta airport, the busiest airport in the world, we had arranged for Alison's college roommate, Katherine Huffman, to meet her and escort her between terminals. Katherine is a brilliant student and a Yale law graduate but she had the dates wrong so Amina was left in the busiest airport in the world looking around for the person who was to meet her. Fortunately, having lived through a war, she was up to the challenge and, with the help of a kind fellow traveler, she arrived in Melbourne on time. I must say, however, that when she deplaned in Melbourne, I think that she was kind of shell-shocked from all of the experiences. Everyone in our family immediately was charmed by Amina and she and Wendy quickly developed a relationship that was much more than friendship. Amina, as I had anticipated, quickly charmed everyone she met and excelled academically. The community college dropped all academic restrictions within a few days and she graduated with honors in about a year and a half. One fortuitous development was that Amina began riding to classes in Cocoa with Kathy Cobb who was then a vice-president at the college. Amina and Kathy quickly became fast friends and confidants, a mutually beneficial relationship. She then entered Florida Tech from which she again graduated with honors. For our family, having Amina with us was a great experience from which we learned much. When she graduated from Florida Tech in May, 2002, she returned to BiH but we were not separated for long.

I actually returned to BiH before Amina returned home for summer vacation after her first year of school in the U.S. In April of 1999, the Air Force deployed me to Sarajevo as part of SFOR. I was assigned to the Office of the High Representative (OHR) for a tour of 6 months. My primary assignment was to lead the international effort to restore the civil aviation system in BiH. I, of course, had no idea that this would be only my first stint with OHR and that I would return as a civilian with a much broader portfolio. In April, 1999, I flew first to Frankfurt, Germany, and Rhine Main Air Force Base. The original plan was that I would fly on military aircraft from there to Sarajevo. However, a few weeks before I arrived in Germany, NATO had begun bombing the Serbs in reaction to the Serb's actions in Kosovo. In order to bomb Serbia, NATO aircraft were overflying the airspace in BiH so the airspace was closed to all non-combat aircraft. Thus, we flew by commercial aircraft from Frankfurt to Zagreb where we were met by a car from OHR which drove us to Sarajevo. At Rhine Main, I had met several other ANG JAG's who were also headed to Sarajevo to work at OHR. Lieutenant Colonel Chuck Tucker was with the Illinois ANG, Major Tim Mullens with the Massachusetts ANG and another major from the Oklahoma ANG. We arrived in Sarajevo and were taken to a building where SFOR troops were housed in the downtown area, mere steps away from the bridge where Archduke Ferdinand had been assassinated in 1913, leading to the outbreak of World War I. Since the building was overflowing, we were all assigned to one room in the basement which we later learned had been a morgue during the war. There was no bathroom in the basement so we had to walk up one floor for the bathroom. We were in that room for a couple of weeks before they relocated me to a room on the second floor which I shared with Lieutenant Colonel Tucker. Since I was the highest-ranking officer in the building, rank definitely did not have its privileges. At OHR, I was in the Military Cell along with a British Vice-Admiral, two British Majors, a British Sergeant, an American Lieutenant Colonel and an American Major. I soon became close friends with the two British Majors, Andy Smith and Hew Williams. I also soon found out that Hew and Andy had an apartment in town which was much more comfortable than my room in the barracks so I moved into their extra bedroom, although I was technically not authorized to move from my assigned barracks. They were extremely kind to me and we spent a lot of time together and developed a close relationship, close enough that the following summer, Wendy, Carrie and I attended Hew's wedding in Great Britain. Among those working with me on civil aviation matters were Vijay Singh, the representative of the International Civil Aviation Organization (ICAO) and General Tony Pilotto, an Italian Air Force General who was the NATO representative. Vijay and Tony became close friends and we have remained in contact in the ensuing years. Vijay has visited us in Florida and we have visited him in Montreal. We had many intrigues as we worked to rebuild the aviation system despite the roadblocks consistently placed in our way by the feuding ethnic groups. We were determined to build a system at the state level (we would describe it as the federal level) while the ethnic groups were determined to avoid any state-level agency. At one point, we found that the Bosniacs (Muslims) in the Bosniac-Croat entity were trying to build their own air traffic control system so that they could have an air-defense system for use against the Serb entity (the RS). We had endless contentious negotiating and drafting sessions and painful discussions with various members of the Parliament but, against all odds, we were finally able to have a bill enacted which formed a civil aviation agency at the federal level. This was the first time since the war that the Parliament had enacted a law creating a federal government level agency. At the same time, we were negotiating with Eurocontrol to have BiH integrate its air traffic control system with the rest of Europe. We were successful in that effort as well. The air war in Kosovo ended with the Serb capitulation and by late summer we were able to reopen air space in BiH for civil aviation. Before ending my deployment, I also became involved in issues relating to the reestablishment of the Bosnian military and also an intelligence service. My friend from Montana, Chip Erdmann, was working in OHR as head of the Human Rights Department at that time so Chip and I spent a lot of time together, including a couple of weekends in Dubrovnik on the Dalmatian Coast.

In August of that year, Wendy, Andy and Carrie flew to Sarajevo and I took a week to be with them. That, too, was unauthorized as BiH was technically a hazardous duty zone in which dependents were not allowed. We managed to avoid anyone who would have cared and we had a nice time, first in Sarajevo and then spent a night in Mali Ston, a charming fishing village on the Adriatic Sea in Croatia, and then a few nights in Dubrovnik. From there, we drove to Gradacac to spend a couple of nights with Amina, who was home for the summer break, and her family. Needless to say, their hospitality was overwhelming. We met all of her family, including aunts, uncles, cousins and grandmothers. Not surprisingly, they were a remarkable family of loving people. Perhaps most remarkable were her grandmothers who were spry and energetic as well as engaging. I detected that there was some controversy among some of her family members as to whether she should return to the U.S. because of her mother's health problems.

In late September, I returned to the U.S. and, after a short fishing trip to Colorado with Homer Denius, I rejoined Holland & Knight which had moved to a new office overlooking the Indian River in my absence. I managed to avoid the pain of the move but Wendy had done most of the work of moving in my absence.

My retirement from the Air National Guard was a big event for me in 2000. I had served 34 years in the organization and it had become an important part of my life. During the last few years of my service, I spent a good deal of my time on ANG matters, traveling throughout the state and nation on military business. I attended the NATO School in Oberammergau, Germany. I also sat as a military judge on several occasions. The last military trial over which I presided was at MacDill Air Force Base wherein the defendant was a Tech Sergeant who had tested positive for drugs in a random urine test. The panel that heard the case were all senior officers. As I sat there and listened to the defendant and his wife concoct an outrageously incredulous story about why he tested positive, I listed at least a dozen inconsistencies in their stories. Imagine my astonishment when the trial panel of senior military officers bought their stories without reservation. After the verdict, a couple of members of the panel asked me if they had done the right thing. I shared my list of inconsistencies with them and they, of course, completely changed their view of the case. This experience only confirmed my view that jury trials are a roll of the dice and that even a jury of military officers will make a decision based upon emotions rather than logic. As a lawyer, I always wanted a jury trial if I thought I had a weak case and a non-jury trial if I had a strong case.

I was somewhat disappointed that I was not promoted to Brigadier General after twice having been recommended for such promotion but I understood that those promotions are quite political. On the second occasion, Lieutenant General Weaver, the Chief of the National Guard Bureau who came from the New York ANG, directly promised Brigadier General Burnett that I would be appointed as the senior ANG Judge Advocate, a two-star position, only to appoint the New York JAG who was widely disliked by most ANG JAG's. The consolation for me was that I would not have been able to go to BiH if I had been promoted to a general officer billet. On balance, the wonderful experiences that I had in BiH far outweighed the benefits of a promotion. Moreover, the position which I would eventually achieve in BiH as a civilian was the civilian equivalent of a two-star military position.

In 2000, I again returned to BiH as an international election supervisor, this time serving in Sarajevo which I now knew well from my time serving in the Military Cell at OHR. In 2001, I was called upon to serve again as an election supervisor, this time in Kosovo. For the Kosovo assignment, I flew first to Skopje, Macedonia (now called North Macedonia in deference to the Greeks), from where we went by bus to a hotel on Lake Ohrid on the Macedonia-Albania border. After training at Lake Ohrid, we went by bus to Kosovo. My first vivid impression of Kosovo was that it was badly polluted. When we reached about 20 KM from the border, we could see this huge yellow-gray cloud of polluted air which seemed to overhang all of Kosovo. Kosovo was much less developed than BiH and the destruction was at least as bad as I had witnessed during my first visit to BiH. The other notable thing about Kosovo was the intensity of the hatred that the ethnic Albanians expressed for the Serbs. Even the ethnic Albanians who were employed by the United Nations and other international organizations openly expressed their hatred for the Serbs, usually in crudely vulgar terms. My translator was a middle-aged man who was very hospitable to me but spent most of our time together trying to convince me to get his ten-year old son out of the country. I was frustrated that all that I could do to help with that is write a couple of letters to international relief organizations. One experience there reinforced my view of the ineptitude of OSCE. The polling station which I supervised was in a remote village. When I arrived at the station, the poll workers had already raised an Albanian flag over the building. The Albanian flag was a prohibited symbol of ethnic nationalism which was intended only to intimidate Serbs who might want to vote at that station. I spent over an hour in touchy discussions with the local poll workers, during which I felt a bit insecure because they were very emotional about it and I was the only international worker present. Finally, after much effort, I persuaded them to remove the flag. A couple of hours later, an OSCE official came to view the voting and the poll workers complained to him that I had required them to remove the flag. He immediately caved in and let them restore the flag, even though it was OSCE which had promulgated the rule forbidding it. That, to me, was illustrative of the lack of backbone and competency of many of these bureaucratic international organizations.

Sarajevo - the author's house is in the lower right-hand corner.
The bridge where Archduke Ferdinand was assassinated is in the center of the photo.

Photo by William C. Potter

Mehmed Paša Sokolović Bridge
This bridge is the subject of Ivo Andric's Nobel Prize-winning novel *The Bridge on the Drina*.

Photo by William C. Potter

Sarajevo

■ AND EXPERIENCES IN BOSNIA and HERZEGOVINA
NOT INCLUDED IN *A BOSNIAN DIARY*

I arrived in Sarajevo in August, 2002. Wendy joined me about a month later. We rented the ground floor of a stately Austro-Hungarian era house near the center of town between the Swiss Embassy and the Vatican Embassy. Within 3 blocks of our house were a mosque, a Jewish synagogue, a Catholic church and an Eastern Orthodox church, symbols of the religious tolerance for which Sarajevo had once been known. We immediately became unusually busy. My work was almost overwhelming and from the outset my typical work day began around 7 AM and often lasted until 8 or 9 in the evening. Wendy immediately made many friends and became active in several organizations, including the International Women's Club which included spouses of most of the ambassadors in the country. Within a few months of our arrival, Amina, who had graduated from FIT and returned to BiH, obtained a job with SFOR at it main base in Butmir, near Sarajevo, and moved in with us. The Bosnian ex-pat with whom she had developed a relationship in the U.S. obtained a job with the U.S. Army as a translator and was soon in Sarajevo as well. Later, Amina was hired as a deputy clerk by the State Court which we had established, a role in which she quickly distinguished herself.

Although my work was consuming, we were able to return to the U.S. frequently to see our family. We were able to return to Florida for Christmas in 2002 and spend time with our family. On our way back to Sarajevo, we stopped in Washington D.C. for a few days where I gave one of the speeches during the ceremony investing Chip Erdmann as a judge of the Court of Appeals for the Armed Forces. And our family visited us as well. Andy and his friend from college, Mitch Fairfield, came to Sarajevo, stayed with us and traveled to Croatia. Carrie came to Sarajevo once and, on another occasion, we met her in Barcelona for several days. Alison, pregnant with Wil, brought Laura and Davis to Munich, from where we took the train to Garmisch in the Bavarian Alps where we spent a week at a ski resort. My brother George and his wife Donna visited us for several days. Wendy's sister Marcia visited and her husband Jim actually worked with OHR for several weeks.

Early in our stay in BiH, I went to The Hague a couple of times to negotiate with the International Criminal Tribunal for Yugoslavia (ICTY) regarding the transfer of war crimes cases from ICTY to Sarajevo for prosecution in our new state court. These discussions and the transfer of these cases are described in *A Bosnian Diary*. Wendy accompanied me on our first visit and both of us had an opportunity to observe the trial of Slobodan Milosevic which was being tried at the time of our visit. It was an eerie feeling to sit in that courtroom in the presence of a man who was pure evil. It was discouraging to see his efforts to intimidate the judges. I knew several judges who could have handled him much better than the ICTY judges did.

One activity that we found enjoyable was hiking in remote parts of the country. There was a company named "Green Visions," founded by a young American graduate of Florida State University, which conducted eco-tours and historical tours of BiH. Because there were still more than 2 million landmines around the country, it was not advisable to leave the roads without someone who knew where mines had been laid. We took several hikes led by the guides from Green Visions and were able to experience the spectacular natural beauty of the Bosnian mountains and visit remote villages where life existed much as it had for hundreds of years.

Speaking of landmines, there was a 4-hole golf course, of sorts, outside of Sarajevo overlooking the city. The problem was that it was surrounded by minefields as denoted by the florescent orange tape warning "Achtung minen." We played the course a couple of times and were amazed that, despite the orange tape surrounding the course, there were golfers over in the minefield retrieving errant balls.

Wendy and I spent one Saturday at a conference of the widows and mothers of Srebenica. Paddy had been asked to attend but he was simply emotionally spent and asked me and Wendy to attend instead. I think that he was particularly keen to have Wendy there on the assumption that her presence might be more soothing to these grieving and emotional women. These were, of course, the widows and mothers of some of the 8,500 men and boys who had been murdered at Srebenica. They were, of course, disgusted and dissatisfied by the efforts of the international community to bring to justice the perpetrators of these murders. In particular, Radovan Karadzic, the President of the Bosnian Serb republic during the war, and Ratko Mladic, the Chief of Staff of the Bosnian Serb Army, were still at-large despite the U.S. and U.K. special forces who were chasing them. The widows and mothers were, not surprisingly, very emotional and we were greatly moved by their pleas. Of course, Karadzic and Mladic were not captured for several more years but were eventually tried and convicted in The Hague.

Since I was paid by an international organization, a portion of my salary and all of my housing allowance were not subject to U.S. income taxes, so long as I did not spend more than 36 days per year in the U.S. Thus, a couple of times we met family or friends in Canada or the Bahamas in order to avoid overstaying our limit in the U.S. During one of our visits, Wendy's older sister Shari tragically and unexpectedly died from sepsis after the recurrence of melanoma which had been diagnosed 7 years earlier. That was a great blow to all of us as Shari was a charming and engaging person who left 2 daughters and 4 grandchildren. No one was prepared to lose Shari at such a young age.

One notable event when we were travelling occurred in London on Remembrance Day, November 11, 2003. I had been invited to speak at a conference held at Wilton Park, a conference center owned by the British Foreign Office in a small village south of London. We spent the night of November 10 in London at the Royal Horseguards Hotel, a block or two from Whitehall, the headquarters of the British War Office. We were oblivious to the fact that the following day was Remembrance Day, commemorating the end of World War I. To our surprise, we discovered the next morning that more than 10,000 British military veterans were gathered to march past Whitehall and that the Queen would lay a wreath on a memorial in front of the building. It was a magnificent parade, led by 3 veterans, ages 103, 103 and 104, who had fought in both world wars. It included a variety of military units, from Nepalese Gurkhas to the Women's Land Army to the Irish Guards. One could not help but feel as they marched by that these were the people who had saved the free world from Fascism. As the bells began to ring throughout London at 11 AM on the 11th day of the 11th month and the Queen began to lay the wreath, my cell phone rang. It was Paddy who assumed that I was in my office one floor beneath his office in Sarajevo. When I informed him that I was in London and could not talk because the Queen was laying the wreath, he informed me that he had laid a wreath on this occasion a few years before. It was an unusually moving experience to see all of these men and women to whom the world owed so much decked out in their formal clothes with rows of medals.

I had a somewhat amusing incident when Senator Bill Nelson (now NASA Administrator) and his wife Grace came to Sarajevo. At our morning meeting, Paddy had told me that he had a meeting with Bill scheduled that afternoon. When I told Paddy that I had known Bill for many years, he asked me to join the meeting. I arrived at the conference room before Paddy and, thus, when Bill and Grace walked in, there I sat instead of Paddy. It took Bill several seconds to recover from the surprise since he had no idea that I was in BiH. We had a cordial meeting, much of which was marked by Paddy and me trying to correct Bill's pronunciation of the names of local officials who he was scheduled to meet.

Another renewed acquaintance that I experienced was with Richard Holbrooke, my classmate from Brown and the architect of the Dayton Peace Agreement. When I confronted Holbrooke just as we were about to go into a meeting, he seemed shocked to learn that I was now an official of OHR and, in typical Holbrooke fashion, acted with what might be interpreted as disdain. I interpreted his response as telling me that OHR must have gone to Hell if I was working there. It really didn't bother me much because he was infamous for being rude and condescending. I felt even better about it when, years later, I learned that when President Obama met him and addressed him as "Dick," he told Obama that he preferred to be called "Richard." That is why we were not particularly friendly at Brown.

Another wonderful event which we were privileged to share was Amina's wedding. Amina and Jasmin Raznica, the ex-pat Bosnian refugee she had met on-line while in the U.S., were married in a religious ceremony in Gradacac and, later that same day, in a civil ceremony in Sarajevo. Wendy and I were their witnesses at both ceremonies. I was a bit apprehensive about the Muslim ceremony due to my concern that I might do something offensive at the mosque, but the Imam was most welcoming and gracious to us. Under their customs, the bride's parents do not participate in either ceremony so that was kind of sad for us. At the civil ceremony in Sarajevo, Wendy and I had to sign the marriage registration book which had been brought to the ceremony by the clerk who I had previously threatened to have fired because she had continually raised obstructions to issuance of the marriage license, a typical bureaucratic ploy by these formerly communist officials who raise these obstacles in hopes of eliciting a bribe. The clerk was notably cool to me but offered no further resistance. The only faux pas that I made was during the toast to the couple when I unthinkingly disclosed that they had met on-line. When I asked Amina whether her family had previously known that, she replied that she did not know if they had been aware but that they certainly knew it now. It was a great privilege for Wendy and me to play roles in their marriage.

I had originally agreed to take the position in BiH until the end of 2003. However, I was engrossed in several projects which I wanted to see to conclusion and Paddy asked me to remain for at least another year. I told him that I would need to take a lot of time away since I had one daughter graduating from college in 2004 and another expecting a baby that year. He told me to feel free to take whatever time was needed. Thus, we returned to the U.S. in May, 2004, for Carrie's graduation from Furman University. Wendy remained in the U.S. to assist Alison who was in the final months of her pregnancy. Wil was born on July 5, 2004, and I arrived home the following day. I returned to BiH a few days later but Wendy remained in the U.S. She remained long enough to experience the 4 hurricanes that hit Florida that year. During one of those hurricanes, power was lost so they had difficulty receiving news while I was 6000 miles away watching the Weather Channel on Armed Forces TV while they broadcast from Melbourne harbor. During another of the hurricanes, Wendy went to Montana and looked for real estate, since we had recently sold several rental properties that we owned. Fortunately, Wendy had closed those sales only a few days before the hurricanes hit. During her trip to Red Lodge, she purchased our house in Red Lodge. She did e-mail me some photos before buying it. After Wendy returned to Sarajevo in the fall of 2004, I began following the Red Sox in the playoffs. In order to watch those games on Armed Forces TV, I had to get up about 2 AM. The games would last until about 5 AM, after which I would rise at about 6 AM in order to get to the office by 7AM. The Red Sox won the first playoff series and faced the Yankees in the American League Championship Series. I dutifully watched the first 3 games, all of which the Yankees won. I then reconciled myself to the fact that this was another agonizing year for Red Sox fans and resolved not to watch again. When the Red Sox miraculously won the next 3 games, I was sure that they were only setting their fans up for another painful disappointment. I was determined that I would not endure the agony of another game 7 defeat so went to bed early that night so that I would not have to bear it. Finally, about 4 AM, I could no longer resist and arose to turn on the television. It was in the 8th inning. Although the score was not immediately apparent, when the camera panned both dugouts, it was obvious that the Red Sox had pulled off the greatest comeback in baseball history. Unfortunately, when the Red Sox swept the Cardinals in the World Series, we were in Brussels where I had some meetings and our only report of the series were a few paragraphs each day in the *International Herald Tribune*. However, my deputy knew that I was an avid Red Sox fan and had a video of the series waiting for me on our return to Sarajevo. I had often wondered whether the Red Sox would win a World Series during my lifetime. I never would have guessed that they would win 4 within a period of 15 years.

We left Sarajevo in February, 2005. Paddy hosted a wonderful departure dinner for my closest associates. I took care to have Amina seated next to Paddy as I knew that they would have great conversations. Wendy and I hosted a reception at a local restaurant which several hundred people attended, including international officials and local officials. One of the touching incidents at the reception was that Zlatco Miletic, the head of the

Federation Police, actually cried as we said good-by. The EU ambassador was particularly gracious, which was surprising because EU representatives rarely speak well of Americans. Paddy actually came to the airport to see us off, something that I had never known him to do before. If I had one regret in leaving, it was that I did not remain until Paddy left in December, 2005. I have sometimes wondered whether I could have pushed through police reform, the last remaining obstacle to EU accession, if I had remained. There was a new U.S. ambassador who was a University of Michigan graduate and I might have been able to develop better relationships with the embassy. But I was tired and Wendy had been more than patient. After Paddy left BiH, the European Union became the dominant player in the international efforts there. The EU had been quite critical of our efforts, asserting that we were too heavy-handed in implementing reforms and that we should allow the Bosnians to decide for themselves and learn from their own mistakes. In my view, such protestations by the EU were naïve and ignored the fact that the Bosnians, left to their own devices, would agree on nothing and even, perhaps, resort to renewed violence. The ensuing years have demonstrated that the EU's benign approach does not work and has brought the country once more to the brink of chaos.

We left BiH with more luggage than we could manage and we also shipped 10 boxes of items accumulated during our residence in Sarajevo. We flew from Sarajevo to Montana where we bought furniture and supplies for our house in Red Lodge and, thus, began a new phase of our lives. We also bought Pas, a red merle border collie who would become a wonderful addition to our family. On our way from Montana to Florida, we stopped to change planes in Salt Lake City and I noticed that one of the workers in the airport had a Bosnian name so I asked her for the Bosnian word for "dog." Thus, Pas acquired her name.

Shortly after I left Sarajevo, one of the major cases that we had undertaken to attack government corruption came to trial. We had arrested and charged Ante Jelevic, a former member of the Bosnian Tri-Presidency and had charged him with multiple counts of corruption arising from his misappropriation of public funds while he was an official of the Federation of Bosnia and Herzegovina. This was a case which drew the attention of the world press. John McNair, a Canadian who we had hired a couple of years previously, did a masterful job of putting together this case and presenting it. The trial had commenced prior to my departure but concluded after I had returned to the U.S. Jelavic was convicted on multiple counts and sentenced to serve 14 years. Unfortunately, he was released pending appeal and he escaped to Croatia. Croatia, as it does with all Croats, refused to extradite him. The only consolation was that shortly after he fled to Croatia, he was kidnapped and held for ransom so his family may have had to use some of the funds he had stolen in order to pay ransom.

Bill and Wendy Potter hiking in Lukomir, a remote mountain village in Bosnia and Herzegovina. Photo by unknown Bosnian.

Commencement Address

Holy Trinity Episcopal Academy, May 2010.

I greatly appreciate the invitation to share this day with you, a day which marks a significant milestone in your lives. Please accept my warmest congratulations to all of you graduates and to your families whose support and love have contributed to your success. You have been the beneficiaries of a unique educational experience at Holy Trinity which has given you a myriad of opportunities to develop your mind, body and spirit. To your great credit, you have seized those opportunities and used them to full advantage, as demonstrated by the fact that there are eight national merit finalists in this class, that ninety percent of you have qualified for Bright Futures scholarships and as shown by your remarkable record of community service and your extraordinary athletic accomplishments.

In thinking about what I would like to say to you today, I reflected upon whether I really had anything of value to impart. It caused me to consider whether simply living long enough is sufficient to claim possession of knowledge worth conveying. I took some solace in a recent University of Michigan study which concluded that there are some cognitive functions which actually improve as one ages. However, my enthusiasm for the study was somewhat tempered by the fact that the chief researcher was 27 years old. In any event, I will leave it for you to determine whether I have anything useful to say. But that question, in turn, caused me to consider the legacy that my generation and the generation of your parents are leaving you. As I pondered what it is that we are passing down to you, I realized that a lot of it is not very encouraging. In fact, a lot of the world which you will inherit is quite daunting. After all, we're passing you a world in which our country has a huge national debt which cannot be sustained without substantially changing our tax system and curtailing significant government programs. We will leave you with a Social Security system that will become insolvent without systemic changes. We are passing on a health care system that cannot be sustained with our rapidly aging population unless we change the way we deliver health care and the way we pay for health care. We have yet to develop an energy policy that will lessen our dependence on foreign oil which causes us great economic, social, environmental and national security problems. The public education system is failing to prepare many of our students to compete in the global economy. In many sectors of our commerce, greed seems to have overcome reason. We leave you with a dangerous, unpredictable world in which both state and non-state actors can threaten us with a variety of horrific weapons. And we leave you with Tom Friedman's "flat world" in which you must compete with all of those Chinese, Indians, Brazilians, Koreans and others who are working diligently to seize the technological lead from the U.S. All of this is bad enough that New York Times columnist David Brooks has called on my generation to lead a "geezers crusade" to demand changes in health care and changes in the retirement system in order to make life better for our grandchildren. And writer

Kurt Andersen has called us the "grasshopper generation" because, like hungry locusts, we have eaten through all the abundance left to us by the greatest generation. Tom Friedman says that we are going to have to replace tooth fairy politics, whereby we tell ourselves that we can have everything without paying a price, with root canal politics. So, I hate to be the bearer of bad news on this day of celebration but you are going to have to figure out the solutions to all of these issues, since my generation has lacked the political will and self-restraint to solve them.

After contemplating all of those depressing problems with which you will have to deal, I almost rewrote the speech because I was ashamed that my generation had not done a better job in managing the world which you enter. And, too, my job today is to inspire you, not to scare the daylights out of you.

However, this dire scenario of these problems which you will inherit is only part of the picture. There is another, more sanguine, view of the society which you will inherit. During the past 15 years, I have spent a considerable time in what are euphemistically referred to as "post-conflict societies"-places like Bosnia, Serbia, Kosovo and Macedonia, places where suffering and conflict of unimaginable proportions had recently occurred and where the average citizen faces only despair and where the young adults face a future without significant opportunity. The most eye-opening lesson for me in working in those places was to learn of their view of the opportunities in the United States. That view was almost universal from a metropolis like Belgrade to the most remote village in Kosovo. Even though the views of our government and our culture might vary greatly depending upon with whom you were talking, their views of the opportunities in our society were uniform. Without exception, people in these post-conflict societies envied the U.S. for the opportunities which it provides. Without exception, they expressed how they envied a society in which one can change one's life through education, hard work, intelligence, imagination and willingness to take risks. I don't know about you but I grew up assuming that most societies rewarded those virtues. Not until I began my experiences in those former Communist countries of eastern Europe did I realize how unique this country is in that respect. I was startled to learn that there are societies throughout the world in which the economic system, the social system and the political system do not allow people to change their lives. No matter how much they gain education, how hard they work, how intelligent they are, how much imagination they have and how much risk they are willing to venture, they are doomed to their predetermined status in life. They are doomed by their ethnicity, their social status, their religion or some other factor that is irrelevant in our society. They are further doomed by the lack of a prevailing rule of law in their society. The lack of a rule of law allows political corruption and organized criminal activity to dominate their society. Without the rule of law, legitimate economic activity and lawful commerce cannot take place and citizens are stuck helplessly in the social and economic status to which they were born.

That is one reason that the U.S. remains a magnet for immigrants. As a result, half of the world's skilled immigrants come to this country and that is why, during the past 20 years, one-fourth of all new venture companies in the U.S. were founded by immigrants. That is why, despite all of the gloomy concerns about our economy, the U.S. remains at the top of every global measure of economic competitiveness. That is why the Rand Corporation recently found that the U.S. continues to lead the world in scientific and technological development and accounts for one-third of the world's research and development spending. And despite the pandering rhetoric of many politicians about jobs being shipped overseas, the U.S.'s share of world manufacturing output has actually increased during the past 20 years. Tom Friedman recently pointed out in another op-ed in the N.Y. Times that between 1980 and 2005, nearly all net new jobs in the U.S. were created by firms that were less than 5 years old. That means that the established firms created almost no new net jobs during that period. That is why Friedman says we need start-ups, not bailouts. This demonstrates the innovation and entrepreneurship that remain the hallmark of our society.

The U.S. is also leading what David Brooks calls a "global age of social entrepreneurship." He points out that in 1964, there were 15,000 foundations in the U.S. Now there are more than 65,000. Total private charitable giving in the U.S. passed $300 billion in 2007.

So, although we have left you with the litany of problems that I recited earlier, we have also left you with a society that rewards accomplishment and encourages initiative and innovation. We have also left you with a society that is compassionate and which encourages social responsibility.

At first blush, these attributes of our society, entrepreneurship and compassion, might seem to be contradictory in some ways. After all, the innovation and opportunity for upward mobility promised by our society are based upon individualism. That is really one of the fundamental values of our society. The Bill of Rights promotes individual choices and, contrary to many societies, admonishes the state, the government, to leave those choices to us. We make individual choices about our religion, our speech, our thought. Our economic system is designed to keep the state out of the process except for the limited circumstances where the public good is direly threatened by unregulated individual conduct. That individualism is an important reason that our society has prospered and an important reason that freedom is so valued in our country and our society. Other societies are much more willing to cede that individualism to the state and allow governments to make many more decisions for them-from planning the economy to telling them what work they will do, to even telling them how many children they can have. Thus, it is important that we retain our individualistic ideals.

However, individualism does not mean that we cannot become part of something greater than ourselves. It is only by being part of some cause or some organization that transcends our individual goals that we truly fulfill ourselves and reach our ultimate potential. In the Air Force where I spent a significant part of my life, it is expressed as a core value of "service above self." That is why our military can take people of previously modest accomplishments and inspire them to do great things. The military imbues them with a sense of responsibility to someone beyond themselves. For many of these military members, it is the first time in their lives that they realize the sense of fulfillment by being part of something that is more important than their individual needs or wants. One of the great heroes of American history was Joshua Chamberlain, the professor from Bowdoin College in Maine who won the Medal of Honor for his bravery in holding the flank at Little Round Top at the Battle of Gettysburg in 1863. Chamberlain, who later became president of Bowdoin and a four-term Governor of Maine, said:

> *It is something great and greatening to cherish an ideal, to act in the light of the truth that is far away and far above; to set aside the near advantage, the momentary pleasure . . . and to act for remoter ends, for higher good, and for interests other than our own.*

Mrs. Ford told me that you are an unusually accomplished class with extraordinary academic accomplishments and great leadership skills. Thank goodness, because we need those skills immediately. All of those problems about energy and health care and deficits and education will not be solved by your elders, so you are going to have to solve them. They can only be addressed if you are willing to subordinate your egos, your interests and sometimes even your opinions to a greater goal. They can only be solved if you are willing to do what modern politicians seem unable to do and engage in a civil discourse which seeks to solve problems and respects differing opinions rather than exacerbating differences. They can be solved only if your generation is willing to make some short term sacrifices in exchange for long term gains, something my generation has been unwilling to do. They can be solved only if you bring to the task all of your imagination and innovative skills but also your sense of compassion and willingness to dedicate yourselves to a cause greater than your individual goals.

I have three grandchildren, all students at Holy Trinity, ages 11, 9 and 5. I often worry about the world that I am leaving for them. It is comforting to know that you are about to contribute your intellect, innovation and compassion to help make a better world for them.

Congratulations, best wishes for continued success and thanks for helping my grandchildren.

An Afternoon with the Kid

This piece was originally written in 2006, but I have continued to enjoy it.

Ted Williams
Photo Source: Public Domain

I recently read a book by the late David Halberstam entitled "Everything They Had: Sports Writing from David Halberstam." Halberstam, who died in an automobile accident in 2007, was arguably the best American journalist of his generation. The books that he wrote about his times such as his Vietnam classic "The Best and the Brightest" or his chronicle of the civil rights movement "The Children," had an enormous impact upon the way Americans perceive our society. Less known but equally as entertaining were his numerous books about modern sports, such as "Summer of '49" describing the classic Red Sox-Yankees baseball pennant race of that year or "The Amateurs" which chronicled the sacrifices and dedication of amateur rowers. Not only were these books about sports entertaining but they were, like his other books about our times, the kind of books that allow us to understand how we have evolved as a nation and as a society and why we think and act as we do today. "Everything They Had," published after Halberstam's untimely death, is a collection of stories written by Halberstam over a period of more than thirty years about sports figures and sports events that strongly impacted our society. These writings provide an instructive look at how our society has evolved in many ways, including in terms of our race relations, our economics and our politics. Most importantly, they are illustrative of the manner in which our fascination with sports has affected our values as a nation and a society.

One of the stories contained in this collection is entitled "My Dinner with Theodore," written in 1990 after Halberstam met and interviewed the great slugger Ted Williams. This recollection was originally published in "Ted Williams: A Portrait in Words and Pictures." The article described not only Halberstam's sense of awe upon meeting Williams but how utterly charming, if slightly profane, Williams could be with his guests. Upon reading this recollection, I was struck by the fact that I had a similar experience with Williams during the year 2000 and left that experience with impressions remarkably similar to those of Halberstam. That thought caused me to want to preserve my memories of the meeting with Williams by writing this article.

I grew up in Michigan during the 1940's and 50's. Television did not appear in most homes until the early 50's. Neither professional basketball nor professional football attracted much attention. Although college football drew hordes of fans, the summer was dominated by major league baseball. My recollection is that it was a rare day in the summertime when our radio was not tuned to Van Patrick and the Tigers. Once or twice each year, we would make the journey to Detroit to watch the Tigers play at their home field of Briggs Stadium. I began as a dutiful son, joining my father, grandfather, uncles and older brother in cheering for the Tigers and their stalwarts such as George Kell, Hoot Evers, Johnny Groth and their great pitcher, Hal Newhouser. However, sometime during the late 40's, I fell from grace and switched my allegiance to the Red Sox and Ted Williams. I do not recall specifically the cause of my revolutionary change of loyalty. It may have been a youthful attempt to demonstrate my independence from the outspoken and strongly held opinions of my father and older brother. Then again, it may have resulted simply from frustration over the inability of the Tigers to provide a meaningful challenge to the hated Yankees. In either event, when I made the change, I adopted the Red Sox and Ted Williams with a passion and devotion that caused me to experience great pain for the next fifty years as the Red Sox year after year raised the expectations of their fans only to dash those expectations at each critical moment. Not until 2004 would the frustrations of being a Red Sox fan disappear in one remarkable comeback in the American League Championship Series, followed by a sweep of the World Series. But as a boy in the late 40's and early 50's, I had no idea of the pain that lay ahead. Instead, I basked in the reflected glory provided by Williams and his achievements. Williams was always particularly effective at Briggs Stadium and it was a memorable experience for me to hear all of my relatives grumbling as he humiliated their beloved Tigers by, for example, going seven for eight in a Sunday doubleheader in Detroit. On another occasion, he hit a homerun of such gigantic dimensions that I recall it to be the first ball hit completely outside of Briggs Stadium.

Although Williams was the magnet that drew me to the Red Sox, many of his teammates were also the objects of my youthful adoration. Bobby Doerr, Johnny Pesky, Dom Dimaggio, Mel Parnell and Ellis Kinder were but a few of these heroes who caused me to give my heart to the Red Sox.

My admiration of Williams was not limited to the baseball field. When he went off to Korea during the Korean War, it was a difficult blow for Red Sox fans, but the thought of this Marine fighter pilot flying in combat only added to his image as a larger than life figure. When he crash landed his jet after a combat mission and walked away from the crash, his stature in my eyes grew even larger.

Williams was also, of course, well known as a spokesman for Sears Roebuck and its sporting goods. On at least one occasion, Williams appeared at the annual sporting goods show at the IMA auditorium in my hometown of Flint. His fly casting demonstrations only added to my awe of this man who seemed to be able to master almost any physical challenge. I remember him casting the fly with great accuracy and for great distances with what appeared to be effortless grace. Not surprisingly, he was elected to the International Game Fish Association Hall of Fame and is the only person to be elected to both the IGFA Hall of Fame and the Baseball Hall of Fame.

When I went to college in New England in the late 50's, Williams was nearing the end of his baseball career. However, I was able to see him play in several games at Fenway Park prior to his retirement. The adoration bestowed upon him by those New England fans was infectious to the extent that it increased my admiration for him to even higher levels. There, I first learned of his charitable activities with the Jimmy Fund and the many acts of kindness and charity for which he was known in New England. I was also moved by stories about how Williams always went out of his way to treat with respect the people doing the most menial jobs in the organization. An example of that occurred when he insisted that the club house manager receive a share of the 1946 World Series money. Further evidence of his character was provided during his induction speech at the Baseball Hall of Fame in 1966 when he called upon the hall to appropriately recognize the members of the old Negro League who had been denied the opportunity to compete in the major leagues.

I also recall visiting the Red Sox spring training camp in Winter Haven during the late 70's and early 80's and seeing Williams, retired since 1960, providing batting instruction to young Red Sox hopefuls. I recall my son, probably about age ten at the time, stopping Williams to ask for an autograph while I held my breath in fear that Williams would be offended by that. But I was delighted that, not only did this icon cheerfully sign the autograph, but he asked my son several questions about whether he played baseball and his preferred position. The gruff portrayal of Williams by the Boston media was quickly exposed as sham by the kindness he displayed to my son.

After retirement, Williams moved to the Florida Keys where his reputation as a fisherman assumed legendary proportions. After I moved to Florida in 1965, I often heard stories of his prowess as a fisherman and his friendships with some of the most notable professional fishermen in the country. When I began fly fishing in the early 80's, I had another reason to admire Williams.

During the late 1970's, I began to follow the athletic programs at the Florida Institute of Technology, a small, private engineering and technology university in Melbourne, Florida. Florida Tech plays in the NCAA Division II and in the very competitive Sunshine State Conference. As I became a fan of Florida Tech soccer, basketball and baseball, I had the good fortune to develop a close friendship with a fellow Florida Tech fan and former major league catcher, Andy Seminick. Andy had played in the major leagues from 1943 to 1957, most notably as a star on the 1950 Philadelphia Phillies "Whiz Kids" team that unexpectedly won the National League pennant that year. Following his major league playing career, Andy had managed and scouted in the Phillies' organization for many years, at least once coming very close to managing the big league team. More than ninety of the players that he coached or managed in the minor leagues ultimately played in the major leagues. Andy continued to scout for the Phillies even after he formally retired. When he moved permanently to Melbourne, he took an interest in the fledgling athletic program at Florida Tech and became its first baseball coach. The baseball field bears his name today.

Andy and I spent countless hours over the ensuing twenty years watching Florida Tech athletics. To my delight, we developed a close friendship. Andy was the son of Eastern European immigrants and his father had worked in the mines of West Virginia. Andy was built like the prototype of a major league catcher of his era, broad, rugged and solid as a rock. When I later read stories about the Whiz Kids, I was not surprised to learn that Andy was one of those players whose reputation was that he was tough as nails and relished every confrontation. The story of how he caught the decisive doubleheader of the 1950 season against the Dodgers with a broken bone in his foot after sitting up all night in his hotel room with his foot in a bucket of ice was a classic. The rivalry between the Phillies and the New York Giants that season resulted in numerous brawls and a physical style of play much different from modern baseball. One notable anecdote concerned an incident with Sal Maglie, sardonically nicknamed "the Barber." When Andy first faced Maglie in this game, Maglie, true to his nickname, gave Andy a close shave by hitting him with a pitch. When Andy again came to bat a couple of innings later, Andy carefully laid a bunt down the first base line, requiring Maglie to come off the mound to the first base line to field the ball. This, of course, allowed Andy to barrel into Maglie like a linebacker sacking a quarterback. Maglie's opinion of that encounter was demonstrated a couple of innings later when Andy again laid a bunt down the first base line while Maglie stood stolidly on the mound and watched the ball die a painful death near the line while Andy advanced to first base.

Off the baseball field, however, Andy gave no hint of that aspect of his personality. He was a kind, gentle and soft-spoken man who was unusually gracious in his dealings with others. As we later worked together on various fundraising events for the athletic programs at Florida Tech, his kindness and respect for others became even more apparent. He often arranged for other former major leaguers to join him in those fundraising efforts. Thus, former players such as Elden Auker of the Tigers and Andy's former teammates Robin Roberts and Curt Simmons made appearances for Florida Tech. Andy's charitable impulses and generous nature were further illustrated by the fact that when fans offered to pay him for his autograph, he directed the proceeds to the church of which he was an active member.

As my friendship with Andy grew, he learned of my devotion to the Red Sox and my admiration of Ted Williams. He related to me some of his experiences with Williams and told me of the enormous respect that he held for him. I was surprised that Andy seemed to evidence some of the same reverential awe of Ted that I had expressed.

During the 90's, faced with declining health and advancing age, Williams moved from Islamorada in the Florida Keys to Citrus Hills, a small community in central Florida west of Ocala. A real estate developer, hoping to use Williams to promote his real estate sales, offered Williams a special deal on a home in his development. The other incentive for Williams to move to that area was the promise of developing a museum to honor the great hitters in baseball history. The museum opened in the mid-90's and included many displays featuring Williams and other Red Sox notables, but also included displays featuring other great hitters in baseball history. Each year, Williams would select a few outstanding hitters for induction into the Hitters Hall of Fame at the museum. An annual induction ceremony for the inductees would attract the attendance of many baseball notables. Andy attended for several years and seemed to relish the invitation and the opportunity to mingle with the former players who were his contemporaries. A friend of mine from Ocala, Fred Roberts, was one of the initial members of the Board of Directors of the museum and Fred and Andy became acquainted. Each of them reported to me how much they had enjoyed coming to know each other. For my part, I did my best to subtly ask each of them to finagle an invitation for me to the induction ceremony but I guess that I was too subtle since neither was able to do so. Thus, for several years I was left to be content to hear their description of the events surrounding the induction of the hitters during each of those years as players such as Rod Carew, Tony Gwynn, Willie Mays, Mickey Mantle, Roger Maris, George Brett and Sadaharu Oh were honored.

Both Andy and Fred spoke to me of the strange role played by John Henry Williams in the care of his father. There had been some publicity surrounding John Henry's attempts to market his father through the sale of autographs, photographs and other means. While many felt that John Henry was merely attempting to exploit his father for financial gain, John Henry argued that he was protecting his father from exploitation by others. It was widely reported, for example, that John Henry hovered around his father at all times in order to prevent anyone from obtaining an autograph without payment. At a minimum, John Henry made some significant mistakes in the manner in which he attempted to market his father's fame and associated himself with some people of questionable substance in doing so. My friend Fred even resigned from the board of directors due to his concerns about the actions of John Henry and some of the people brought in by John Henry to participate in these marketing efforts.

In the spring of 2000, Andy called me to ask if I would drive him to visit the museum. He explained that he did not have much opportunity to tour the museum during the induction ceremonies and would like to make a leisurely visit that would enable him to see all of the exhibits. I readily agreed since I was also anxious to see the museum. Thus, we came to make the two hour drive from Melbourne to Citrus Hills.

We arrived at the museum at about 11 A.M. We paid the admission fee and began to tour the museum, studying each display with interest. The museum was quite well done and, for a die hard Red Sox fan like me, was a treasure trove of nostalgia. After we had been examining exhibits for about thirty minutes, a man approached us and introduced himself as the curator of the museum. He then asked Andy whether he was Andy Seminick, the former Phillies catcher. Andy replied affirmatively and they discussed the 1950 National League pennant race for a few minutes, during which it became obvious that the curator was a fount of baseball knowledge. The curator left us shortly after and disappeared into his office. A few minutes later, he returned and informed us that he had called Ted to tell him that Andy was at the museum and Ted wanted us to come up to his house to see him. Andy was delighted to receive the invitation and for me it was like a childhood dream turned to reality. It is notable that the curator warned us not to ask Williams for his autograph, noting that John Henry would be at the house and would be upset if we made such a request. Although I could not discern with certainty whether the curator disapproved of John Henry's action, I had the impression that he did. Since I already possessed several autographs of Williams, I was not disappointed that I would not be able to acquire another. We eagerly left the museum and drove a couple of miles to Williams' house following the directions provided by the curator.

Williams' house sat on a hill on the opposite side of the real estate development from the museum. The road leading to the house was guarded by an electronic gate which was opened remotely as we approached the house, a large ranch style dwelling. We were greeted at the front door by a man who was obviously expecting us. He appeared to be some kind of caregiver to Williams. He immediately showed us into a large kitchen and invited us to sit at a table at the end of the room. Within seconds, Ted Williams shuffled into the room with the aid of a walker. He wore an unbuttoned shirt with a sleeveless undershirt beneath the shirt. One might gain an image of a disheveled, feeble man from that description but that was not the image portrayed to me. Despite the walker and his shuffling walk and despite the unbuttoned shirt, he presented to me the appearance of a large, imposing man with a commanding presence. He greeted Andy with obvious warmth and enthusiasm. When Andy introduced him to me, he seemed friendly and open, not at all reserved in his greeting. That was the beginning of an unforgettable discussion that continued for almost three hours, a discussion to which I was initially only an eager listener but in which I eventually became a frequent participant. As we talked, the caregiver periodically came into the kitchen, ostensibly to check on things in the refrigerator but I suspect also to check on his ward. John Henry did not come into the kitchen during our visit but we could periodically hear him in other parts of the house.

Although Andy and Ted had spent their careers in different leagues, they had numerous encounters during spring training as well as having played against each other in the 1949 All-Star game. Moreover, they had countless mutual friends among the relatively small fraternity of elite athletes who play major league baseball. They began by talking at length about their experiences and the players with whom they had competed, each offering their assessments of the relative talents of these players. In offering these opinions, both Andy and Ted were invariably complimentary and kind in their observations of their contemporaries. Ted was particularly generous in his comments about several of Andy's teammates on the Phillies such as Richie Ashburn, who had died in 1997, and Robin Roberts. Andy reciprocated by talking with great fondness about Ted's Red Sox teammates such as Bobby Doerr and Dom Dimaggio. It became obvious that Ted had felt lonely and isolated by his infirmities and that he was relishing this opportunity to discuss baseball with someone like Andy who could relate to his thoughts in such a meaningful manner. Several times, Andy made polite comments that offered Ted the opportunity to end the visit but Ted hurriedly dismissed such suggestions. Although Ted's speech was sprinkled with mild profanities, they were uttered in such a natural, innocent and unforced way that they were not at all offensive but rather seemed to be contextually appropriate.

The conversation migrated from recollections of specific players to the technicalities of baseball. Ted began describing the best pitchers that he had faced and the attributes that had allowed them to challenge his hitting skills. Then, Ted began to discuss the techniques of batting. Andy's tepid response to this discussion made it clear that Andy had never thought about the art of hitting in quite these terms but relied upon a more instinctive approach to hitting. At one point, Ted asked Andy whether he swung inside-out or outside-in when confronted with an inside curve ball. Andy's response was: "Hell, Ted. I don't know, I just tried to hit it." That exchange seemed to exemplify their differing approaches to the art of hitting a baseball. Ted's face lit up as he spoke about hitting and his passion for the art dominated the room. It was easy to understand why Carl Yastrzemski had said of Williams: "He studied hitting the way a broker studies the stock market."

At some point, Andy mentioned to Ted that I had recently served in the military in Bosnia and Herzegovina. That seemed to interest Ted and he asked me several questions related to my thoughts on the future of Eastern Europe and the former Yugoslavia in particular. He made it obvious that he did not approve of the United States' interventions around the world.

We also spent some time talking about fly fishing. I described to Ted some of the places where I had fished for bonefish such as Christmas Island, the Bahamas and Venezuela. That led Ted to talk about his experiences fishing for bonefish in the Florida Keys and how much he regretted that he was no longer able to do that. I asked him about his experiences in fishing for Atlantic salmon at his cabin on the Miramichi River in New Brunswick, Canada and he responded in a way that indicated his fondness for those recollections and his passion for the sport.

Although we heeded the admonition of the curator about requesting autographs, Andy asked whether Ted was agreeable to taking photographs. Ted seemed happy, even eager, to do so. I took a photograph of Ted and Andy and then Andy reciprocated by taking a photograph of me and Ted.

As we had been speaking, the caregiver had come in several times to work in the kitchen, indicating that he was beginning to prepare dinner. At the mention of dinner, Ted immediately asked us to stay for dinner. The response of the caretaker was to point out that they were having lobster that night and had only enough for three people. We quickly responded that we needed to return home for dinner and would be unable to stay. It seemed obvious to me that the caretaker's concern about us staying for dinner was more a concern from John Henry about how long we had already visited.

In any event, we made our excuses and took our leave shortly after the discussion about dinner. Ted seemed genuinely saddened by our departure. I was left with the strong impression that he was lonely and isolated and eager for companionship but that his son was so protective that he made it difficult for his father to have much social interaction at all. I reserved judgment as to the motivation behind John Henry's protective actions.

Williams, of course, died a couple of years later. He was then subjected to the humiliation of having his children fight over the disposition of his remains. John Henry and Ted's daughter, Claudia, advanced the somewhat bizarre idea that Williams wanted his remains preserved by cryogenics so that he might some day return to life. William's daughter from his first marriage, Barbara Joyce, attempted to thwart this and have his remains disposed of by more conventional means. Their battle over this issue ended up in litigation in which John Henry and Claudia prevailed by virtue of a writing which they alleged had been signed by Ted expressing his wish to be frozen in this manner. Others maintained that Ted had been duped into signing this writing and thought that he was merely signing an autograph. Less than two years later, however, John Henry himself died from leukemia while still in his early thirties.

Williams had always been a controversial figure. His relations with the Boston press were so strained that any defect he had was magnified beyond reality while his many good deeds were hardly reported. Although revered in New England as perhaps the greatest sports figure ever in that region, even in death he could not escape controversy as his children battled over his remains. For me, however, there was no controversy, only a heroic figure who was passionate about all of the endeavors he undertook.

The museum struggled financially after Williams' death. Fortunately, however, the Tampa Bay Rays moved the memorabilia from the museum to their home field at Tropicana Field in Tampa, where it was reconstituted as the Ted Williams Museum and Hitters Hall of Fame. It is open during all of the Rays' games.

My friend Andy Seminick died in February 2004. At the time of his death, he was the last living everyday player from the Whiz Kids team.

Bill Potter (left) and Ted Williams (photo by Andy Seminick)

The Journey of Island Girl

This is my journal of our 2006 sail across the Atlantic Ocean from Cascais, Portugal, to Antigua aboard a 44-foot catamaran.

Tuesday, November 14, 2006

Bob Lindeke and I departed Melbourne at about 0600 EST in order to pick up Scott Bell in Indialantic and, then, Dave Underill in Vero Beach. We arrived at Miami International Airport around 1115 in ample time to check luggage and wait for our departure at 1330. We arrived at Washington Dulles around 1630 where we met the fifth member of our group, Bob Snyder, and transferred to our flight to Frankfurt which departed at 1930.

Wednesday, November 15, 2006

We arrived in Frankfurt at 0730, European Central Time, and departed for Lisbon at 0930, arriving in Lisbon at 1130. After clearing customs, we took two taxicabs about 35 kilometers north of Lisbon to Cascais, where *Island Girl* was moored at a large marina near a 17th Century fortress. It was raining quite hard and the winds were high causing the waves to crash over the seawall surrounding the marina. On arrival at the boat, we met Mike, the representative of The Catamaran Company. Mike informed us that the autopilot on the boat was not working but assured us that he had contacted the manufacturer and that a new motor to repair the autopilot had been shipped.

Dave and Mike began the process of reviewing the checklist of items to be accepted in order for Dave to accept the boat and send the required acceptance documents to the manufacturer. To me, it sounded like a somewhat illogical process in that, as I understood it, Dave had to accept the boat in order to make the warranties effective but yet, by accepting the boat, he was signifying his acceptance of the boat in its current condition. That night, we went with Mike to a nearby restaurant in the older part of Cascais, only about a ten minute walk from the boat, where we had a nice meal and some good local wine.

Thursday, November 16, 2006
The wind was now blowing from the north. Mike took us to a nearby superstore, "Jumbos," where we spent several hundred euros stocking up for the journey. We purchased not only food but also supplies such as plates, blankets, paper supplies, cleaning supplies, fishing poles and a variety of other supplies we would need. It became apparent that the arrival of the motor necessary to repair the autopilot was much less certain than Mike had originally indicated and that we would be here for several days before it was repaired. Dave also arranged for the local Yanmar dealer to service the two diesel engines during which they discovered that the oil in the port engine was too low to register on the dipstick. This was quite worrisome as it caused us to think that there may be a leak in some part of the engine. Tonight, we dined at a small restaurant overlooking the harbor and again had a nice meal with some very reasonably priced local wine. After dinner, Mike departed in order to catch a flight returning to the U.S. early Friday morning.

Friday, November 17, 2006
The wind was now coming out of the northeast at gusts up to 20 knots. Raymarine arrived to inspect the autopilot and confirmed that it needed a new motor. They assured us that the new motor will arrive on Monday morning and that they would be here to install it before noon on Monday. This, of course, means that our departure would be delayed until Monday afternoon. That will probably cause us to sail directly to the Canary Islands rather than stopping at Medeira. We made another of what would evolve into several trips to Jumbos and stocked up on additional supplies. Bob Lindeke and I stopped and had lunch in the old part of town at a small sidewalk restaurant where we had a nice shrimp salad and some good local wine. Tonight, Dave fixed dinner

on the boat where we were joined by Ben Scott, a Dutch accountant from a nearby sailboat. After dinner, Dave, Scott, Ben and Bob Snyder were able to crash a party in the old castle being held to film the debut of a new car model. Bob Lindeke and I showed our ages by staying on the boat and sleeping.

Saturday, November 18, 2006
We made another trip to Jumbos, where we are becoming well recognized figures. We had a nice dinner at a small local restaurant where the husband was the cook and the wife the waitress. After dinner, we went to a nearby bar where we were able to persuade one of the waiters to turn one of the televisions to the Michigan-Ohio State football game. Since none of the other patrons were at all interested in the game, I felt like I needed to keep buying drinks to justify monopolizing the television, so I ended up drinking about six rounds of Scotch and was feeling little pain by the time the game ended. It was a great game despite the outcome and I was able to stagger back to the boat and climb on, so I wasn't too drunk.

Sunday, November 19, 2006
Another trip to Jumbos brought more provisions. I have been accused of overdoing the olives and hot dogs and must admit that perhaps I did get carried away a bit. We also did our laundry and made other preparations for departure, including securing the life raft on the stern. We also reviewed the use of life jackets and prepared them for use. I completed reading John Grisham's The *Innocent Man*, his non-fiction book about a couple of men wrongfully convicted of murder in Oklahoma. It was a fascinating book which I read in less than 24 hours. The wind was quite calm and good weather was predicted for Monday which made our departure appear hopeful.

Monday, November 20, 2006
The Yanmar dealer's crew appeared shortly after 11 A.M. with the needed motor in order to repair the autopilot. True to their promise, they installed it in less than one hour and we prepared to depart. I mailed some postcards while Dave fueled the boat. We departed Cascais at 1220 hours. The winds were 11 knots from the north northeast and the seas about six feet. We scheduled shifts of four hours on and six hours off with two people on the bridge at all times. We resolved to use Greenwich Mean Time (Zulu time) for the journey. We estimated that it would require about 98 hours to sail to La Palma, the westernmost of the Canary Islands.

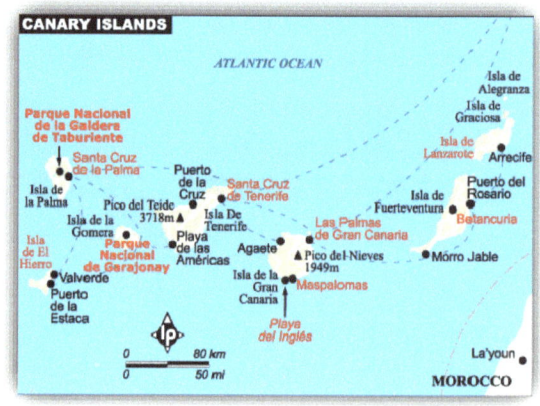

Tuesday, November 21, 2006
During our first 24 hours, we sailed about 170 nautical miles. We were off the coast of Morocco, but too far from land to see it. Winds were about 7 knots. It was my birthday which the crew marked by giving me a "Twinky-like" cake and singing badly.

Wednesday, November 22, 2006

At about 0300, we called Alison and caught Alison, Carrie and the kids at the Newark Airport awaiting a ride to New York City. The kids all wished me happy birthday. We sailed about 160 nautical miles during our second 24 hours at sea. We checked the oil in the port engine and found that, once again, it appeared that it has lost both engine oil and transmission oil. We called Augusto, the Yanmar dealer in Lisbon, who assured us that he would call a man in the Canary Islands. This meant that we would probably divert to an island other than Las Palmas. Later, Augusto called us back and told us that there is a Yanmar technician in Las Palmas on Gran Canary Island so we decided to head there. The only problem with that was the fact that there were a couple of hundred boats at Las Palmas waiting for the start of the Atlantic Rally for Cruisers ("ARC"), a rally for sailboats sailing between Las Palmas and St. Lucia. We expected to arrive in Las Palmas either late Friday or early Saturday. We saw several whales, the closest of which was about 100 meters from the boat. We put out a trolling line behind the boat but had no luck. When we tried to estimate how fast we could expect to make it across, we discussed the fact that Columbus twice crossed in 21 days, remarkable feats when you consider that he was sailing in leaking boats with no engines and only the most primitive navigation equipment. It made our venture seem mundane when you consider the fact that we had five global positioning satellite systems, two diesel engines, a satellite telephone and a host of other electronic marvels.

Thursday, November 23, 2006
We celebrated Thanksgiving with a traditional spaghetti dinner. No pumpkin pie, however. Seas were quite calm with the wind about six knots. We spoke with Wendy, Alison, Carrie and the kids who were enjoying the Macy's parade and other activities in New York.

Friday, November 24, 2006
It was remarkable to be up on the bridge at 0730 as the sun rose over Africa to our portside. The wind had picked up to 18 knots from the south-southwest. Since we were heading almost due south, we were able to make only about six knots per hour even with both engines running. We were about 100 nautical miles from Las Palmas. Later, with the winds at 20 knots directly in our face, we decided to divert to Islas de la Lanzarote because the prevailing winds were much more favorable for that course rather than Gran Canary.

Although Dave was a bit apprehensive about entering an unfamiliar harbor at night, we made it to the marina without problems about 2030, just as it was closing for the day. We took quite a beating most of the day due to the constant choppy seas so the serenity of the marina was welcome. Scott, Bob Lindeke and I had a nice dinner at a restaurant in the marina. The marina, named the Marina Rubicon, was quite new, very large and quite extravagant with nice shops and restaurants. Lanzarote is apparently quite a popular European tourist destination.

Saturday, November 25, 2006

We stayed in Lanzarote for most of the day. We did a little grocery shopping, picked up some crafts at an arts and crafts exhibition held in the marina and did a little sightseeing. There are the remnants of an old chapel on a hill overlooking the marina. The chapel indicates that it was built in 1769 and it is kind of the focal point for some pathways leading to the edge of the cliffs and some viewpoints with nice views of the marina, the sea and some other islands a few kilometers away.

Dave and I took a taxi to a service station a few kilometers from the marina where we bought enough transmission oil to make us comfortable that we will be able to address any concern with the port engine. The bulletin board in the marina office was interesting in that it was filled with messages from people looking to sign on as crew members to cross the Atlantic. We had a pizza dinner at a restaurant in the marina about 1600 in time to set sail for Gran Canary about 1800.

Sunday, November 26, 2006

After a relatively smooth sail, we arrived in Las Palmas on Gran Canary Island at about 0920. Surprisingly, it appeared to be a modern city with a population of several hundred thousand people. Due to the fact that the participants in the ARC were still in port, there were no berths in the marina at the time of our arrival so it was necessary for us to anchor in the harbor outside of the marina. Dave hailed a passing dinghy and hitched a ride to shore to check out the situation.

The ARC began at 1300 so we had a good view of the start of the rally and enjoyed watching the departure of the approximately 250 boats participating in the rally. Apparently there are two parts of the rally, the first of which is the group which actually races to the destination and the second part which is larger and whose participants merely cruise to the destination without competing. The variety of boats participating was quite striking, varying from those that appeared to be professional racers to those that seemed to be surprisingly casual recreational sailors. After the departure of the ARC, we motored into the marina at about 1400, only to find that the marina office was closed and that we could neither purchase fuel or rent a berth for the night. We reacted to that dilemma by merely docking at the fuel dock for the night. We spent some time exploring the restaurants and shops around the marina and had a nice dinner in a nearby restaurant.

Monday, November 27, 2006
Bob Snyder went to the Yanmar dealer to confirm that they would be by to look at the engine but the dealer professed to have no knowledge of our problem and denied that he had received a call about it. By that time, we were convinced that there was really no problem with the oil in the engine but that, for some reason, it simply did not register on the dipstick when one first examined it, so we were not concerned with the apathy of the Yanmar dealer. Dave and I went to a supermarket a few blocks away and stocked up on more food. We also bought a couple of jerry cans for extra fuel as well as more bottled water. We now had enough bottled water for probably 22 days at sea. The additional fuel gave us comfort that we would be able to supplement the sails by running the engines quite frequently, particularly during the second half of the voyage. After refueling and taking a final shower on land, we departed Las Palmas at 1100. We headed west southwest from Gran Canary, heading for latitude 23 north, longitude 25 west.

Tuesday, November 28, 2006
We were sailing west-southwest along the African coast. We made 170 nautical miles during our first 24 hours from Las Palmas. Shifting winds made it a noisy and bumpy ride requiring frequent changes of course. The noise and motion made it very difficult to sleep. We trolled for fish and hooked one which broke our line. In view of the fact that we were using 50-pound test line, it must have been a big fish.

Wednesday, November 29, 2006
We were now sailing almost due west but needed to go quite a bit further south. Right then, we were trying to reach latitude 23 north, longitude 30 west. We needed to reach 23 north latitude or lower in order to pick up the trade winds. The trade winds are a result of the flow of air from the North Atlantic high pressure areas to the permanent low-pressure trough around the equator commonly known as the doldrums. The wind direction is further affected by the rotation of the earth so that the moving air is directed toward the west. At about 1415, we spotted a whale and within a few minutes spotted several porpoises swimming with the boat. At about 1530, we landed a dolphin weighing about five pounds which would at least make a nice appetizer.

Thursday, November 30, 2006
The wind was down to about 10 or 11 knots. We made only about 137 nautical miles during our second 24 hours since leaving Las Palmas. We spoke with Chris Gates who told us that we have now caught up with much of the ARC fleet and will begin passing them in the next couple of days.

Friday, December 1, 2006
We were now north of the Cape Verde Islands and making less than six knots per hour which was disappointing and meant that our crossing might take longer than expected. We were hopeful that the winds would increase and we would be able to make better time. We began discussing the possibility of stopping first at Antigua before continuing to Tortola. Tortola is about a 24 hour sail from Antigua. We caught a small Bonito and a Dolphin which weighed about seven pounds. I fought a Dolphin which weighed between 25 and 20 pounds for about 25 minutes but he broke off when he was about four meters from the boat. At about 2315, we had a school of more than 20 porpoises swim with the boat for about 15 minutes.

Saturday, December 2, 2006
At 0700, we passed the waypoint indicating that we have traveled one-fourth of the distance between Gran Canary Island and the British Virgin Islands. Winds were about 20 knots with high seas. Although we were making more than eight knots, the seas were very tumultuous. Between the choppy seas and the noise of the propeller turning, I found it impossible to sleep in my bunk. There were flying fish all around the boat, some of which periodically landed on the deck. Although Dave was enthusiastic about eating them, I was less enthusiastic. During the day, we

passed a boat from the ARC. We were now west of 25 west and below 23 north. Our hope was that when we reached a point below 20 north, we would have steady westerly winds of more than ten knots which would enable us to have smooth sailing in excess of eight knots.

Sunday, December 3, 2006
We continued to have high seas between ten and fifteen feet. We experienced wind gusts up to 35 knots.

Monday, December 4, 2006
We experienced continued high seas which resulted in slow sailing, only about six knots. At this rate, we could not expect to reach the British Virgin Islands until December 18. We should reach the halfway point between Gran Canary Island and the British Virgin Islands in about two and a half days. Reaching the halfway point would be significant in that it would give us a better gauge of the adequacy of our supplies of food, water and fuel. We spoke with Chris Gates by satellite telephone and he informed us that we were now in the middle of the ARC fleet and that the participants were reporting that these are the roughest seas experienced during the history of the ARC. We also spoke by VHF radio to *Tao-Tao*, a large schooner which departed from Las Palmas after we departed. This schooner was doing ten to twelve knots so was catching up with us. It reported that one of the boats in the ARC has lost a mast while another boat in the fleet had an injured crew member who was evacuated to a large boat with medical facilities.

Tuesday, December 5, 2006
Winds remained at more than twenty knots. Seas remained high and turbulent. We were informed that the seas will likely remain this way for ten or eleven more days. We expected to pass the halfway point tomorrow night. I spoke with Wendy and it appeared that her knee surgery went well.

Wednesday, December 6, 2006
Seas remained ten to fifteen feet and wind gusts up to thirty knots continued. We were informed that one of the ARC boats has been abandoned after the captain went mad and had to be evacuated by helicopter. Another boat in the ARC suffered a broken boom. We were contemplating stopping at Antigua and estimated that we could arrive there on the morning of Friday, December 15. Scott would probably disembark there and I might do so as well. Tortola is

another 150 nautical miles past Antigua. We have now passed the halfway point between Las Palmas and Antigua. The seas remained churning. It was not the height of the waves that was problematical but rather the fact that the seas were so unsettled and came from all directions. Most of the boats in the ARC were now south of us as they head for St. Lucia.

Thursday, December 7, 2006

The seas remained high and "nervous" with the waves coming from all directions. The waves often appeared to be higher than the boat and we often found the boat surfing down the crest of the waves. It is a daunting experience to be sitting on the bridge in the middle of the ocean in the deep of night and to look behind you to see a wave coming up behind that appears to be fifteen or twenty feet higher than the boat. It makes one feel rather helpless and insignificant. Joseph Conrad wrote that "The ocean has the conscienceless temper of a savage autocrat spoiled by much adulation." We calculated that we might be out of the high seas tomorrow. It certainly would be a welcome change to sail without bouncing in all directions as we had for the past nine or ten days. We were now beginning to plan on reaching Antigua on December 15 and Tortola on the 16th. We landed a nice fifteen to twenty-pound Dolphin, which would make a nice dinner. Just before sunset, we were overtaken by the *Mirabella V,* the largest single-mast sailboat in the world. It is about 165 feet in length and carries a crew of thirteen. We spoke with them and they were doing about eleven knots. Although they are behind schedule after stopping to pick up three from a boat in the ARC which was abandoned, they expected to be in Antigua by the 11th. Dave asked if there was anything we could do to help them and they were polite enough not to laugh at us. It is one impressive boat. Scott and Bob Lindeke considered jumping overboard so that they could be rescued by *Mirabella*.

Friday, December 8, 2006

The high seas continued with winds between fifteen and twenty knots. The continued choppy ride and lack of sleep were beginning to wear heavily on me and perhaps on some of the others as well. The stars at night were quite spectacular and the shooting stars were enchanting. It was not unusual to see a dozen shooting stars during a couple of hours on watch during the night.

We spotted a large bird today that Scott surmised was an albatross. An albatross is an amazing bird with a wingspan of as much as twelve feet. It can remain at sea for up to two years without returning to land, sleeping while flying. It may live for sixty or seventy years.

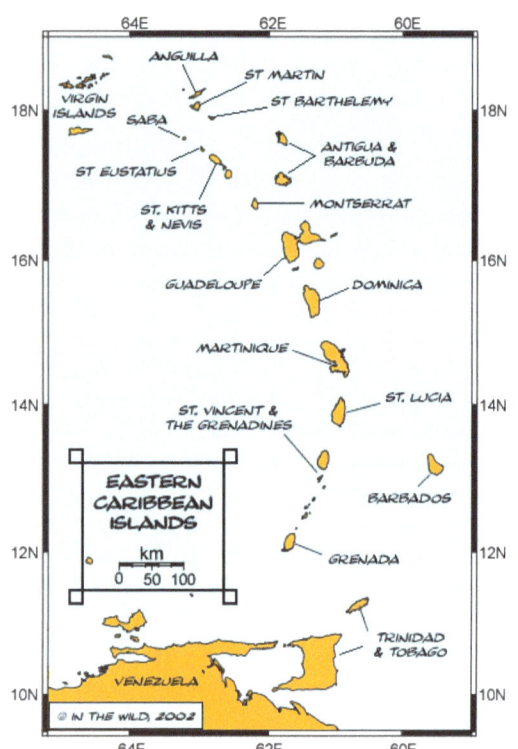

Saturday, December 9, 2006

One of the remarkable observations was to see a brownish hue on parts of the boat and to realize that it was sand from the Sahara Desert blown by the trade winds over one thousand miles out to sea. We were now quite certain that we would stop in Antigua and that Scott and I would disembark there. We had tentative plane reservations for 4 P.M. on Friday. We were now south of the Sargasso Sea and north of The Doldrums. The Sargasso Sea has a unique ecosystem containing sea grasses which support marine life not found elsewhere in the Atlantic.

Sunday, December 10, 2006

We were now trying to calculate whether we could be in the British Virgin Islands by Friday morning. If so, we would probably head directly there rather tan stopping in Antigua. For a while, the seas were down to five to ten feet, but they soon rose again to ten to fifteen. We were now running the engines more than half of the time to assist the sails.

Monday, December 11, 2006

We once again experienced porpoises swimming alongside the boat as they played. The shooting stars were particularly spectacular tonight. We were now planning on landing in Antigua on Thursday afternoon.

Tuesday, December 12, 2006

At 1100, we were 400 nautical miles from Antigua. We caught a ten- to fifteen-pound Dolphin, which we quickly consumed for dinner.

Wednesday, December 13, 2006

I fell asleep on the couch in the salon and gained a better rest than I have had in several days. We made 183 nautical miles towards Antigua during the past 24 hours. We continued to see a lot of shooting stars and flying fish. Although we were continuing to use Greenwich Mean Time ("Zulu"), it is becoming somewhat confusing since we were so far west that it meant that sunrise did not occur until almost 0930 Zulu. We needed to make the switch to Atlantic Time and did so.

Thursday, December 14, 2006

We saw some spectacular rainbows this morning, including a double rainbow where we could see the complete arc of both rainbows. Bob Lindeke spotted Antigua at about 1230 Atlantic Time, the first land we had seen in more than two weeks. As we neared Antigua, we could see *Mirabella V* come out of the harbor together with *Maltese Falcon*, the largest and fastest privately owned sailboat in the world. It was quite a sight to see these two super yachts together. At 1420 Atlantic Time, we entered English Harbor, Antigua. Our first stop was at a fuel dock where we refueled. I jumped off to watch the fuel gauge on the pump. It was a great feeling to walk without staggering. I also took the opportunity to purchase and quickly down a Diet Coke. After fueling, we motored across the harbor to Nelson's dockyard where we moored overnight. It was an adventure getting into the slip as the guys working of the wooden boat next to us panicked for fear that we would scrape their recently completed varnishing job. As soon as we were safely moored, Scott and the two Bobs and I headed for an outdoor bar that was only about twenty meters from the dock. There, we quickly downed about three drinks apiece. For myself, I had three Scotches in about twenty minutes and soon had regained my land legs. Dave, ever the dutiful captain, passed up the drinks in order to square things with the Customs Office. We hooked up the shore water to the boat and all enjoyed full showers for the first time since leaving Las Palmas. English Harbor is an incredibly well-protected natural harbor with an interesting history. It is guarded by British forts on both sides. The forts were built during the seventeenth century and have been used by the British fleet over several centuries. Nelson's Boatyard was a British Naval Yard which was the center of the activities of the British Navy in the Caribbean during the eighteenth and nineteenth centuries. Admiral Lord Nelson spent a lot of time there. It is now a national park of Antigua and Barbuda and has been largely restored and contains lots of historical exhibits. We enjoyed looking at the old buildings and the museum. It was also interesting to watch *Maltese Falcon* back into the harbor where it towered over the rest of the yachts, making these fifty- or sixty-foot yachts appear as if they were mere dinghies. After looking around a bit, we found a local restaurant where the woman appeared to be the waitress, cook and dishwasher. We all enjoyed a nice dinner with some wine. When we returned to the boat, we discovered that there was a party with a band and free food and drinks sponsored by those sponsoring the races between the super yachts. So we then partook of more food and drinks.

Friday, December 15, 2006
We were up at about 0630 and had breakfast at a restaurant on the dock. Dave was anxious to start for Tortola so was off with the two Bobs at about 0830. Although it was somewhat nostalgic to wave farewell to them as they sailed out of the harbor, I think that we were also happy to be heading home to see our families. The previous evening, we had arranged to meet a taxicab at 1000, so Scott and I enjoyed a nice tour of Antigua until about 1300. It is a beautiful island with an interesting history. Once it was very heavily dependent upon cultivating sugar cane and, therefore, heavily dependent upon the slave trade. Now, of course, tourism is the centerpiece of its economy and sailing is a large part of its tourism. We departed Antigua at about 1630, arriving in San Juan about 1800. We went through U.S. Customs in San Juan but our departure was delayed

so we did not leave until about 2200. We arrived in Fort Lauderdale about midnight, Eastern time, where we met Alison and the kids. We drove back to Melbourne, arriving about 3 A.M. on Saturday, December 16.

Epilogue
Winston Churchill once described the traditions of the Royal Navy as "rum, sodomy, and the lash." Samuel Johnson analogized sailing on a ship to being in jail. He said, "No man will be a sailor who has contrivance enough to get himself into a jail, for being in a ship is being in jail, with the chance of being drowned.... A man in jail has more room, better food, and commonly better company." There were times during our voyage when these quotations may have seemed somewhat accurate, although I must quickly add that neither the sodomy nor the "better company" was applicable. However, the lack of room and opportunity for drowning certainly struck a note at times.

Business Hall of Fame
Acceptance Speech

The following is the acceptance speech I gave when I was inducted into the **Space Coast Business Hall of Fame**, March 2016.

Allow me to express my profound thanks for this recognition. It is, indeed, humbling to be recognized with Bill Brown and to join the ranks of past honorees, including so many people who I have admired and respected. I have observed for the past fifty years the positive manner in which our community has been shaped by many of these past honorees and it is a privilege to be associated with them.

I guess the gracious thing for me to do at this point would be to utter a few platitudes about free enterprise and sit down while I am ahead. However, one of the few advantages of advancing age is freedom to express opinions that other people may not be interested in hearing. When you are younger, people just consider you rude but when you reach my age, they attribute it to the onset of dementia. So I beg your indulgence for a few minutes while I exploit this opportunity in order to voice some concerns about the direction of our society.

Junior Achievement has, as you are well aware, the important objective of teaching young people about the workings of the free-market economy and how that economic system benefits our society. When we talk about those benefits, most people think in terms of the material well-being that inures to society from that system. But that really misses the point. The salient point is that free-market economics and the opportunities which flow from that system are the bedrock of democracy and essential to a free society. Without the opportunities for social and economic advancement offered by that economic system, a democratic society cannot endure and true freedom cannot exist. I think that history proves that beyond debate.

Only when I went to Sarajevo and became part of a management team attempting to repair a post-communist, post-conflict society did I really begin to understand the role of market economics in a democracy and a free society. Prior to the brutal war in Bosnia-Herzegovina, that country had existed for 45 years under the heavy-handed rule of Tito's Yugoslavia and communism. What seems obvious now, but what I must confess I had never thought much about, was how the absence of free-market economics and the absence of the opportunities inherent in that system, made a free democratic system impossible. For the essence of free-market economics and the essence of democracy are the same-that is, the opportunity to change one's circumstances in life.

It is an essential requirement of a democratic system and a free society that its citizens be able to change their economic and social status through hard work, education, risk-taking and creativity. What I observed in Bosnia were the results of 45 years when those opportunities were not available. Under communism, the only ways to change one's social and/or economic status in life were through engaging in organized criminal activities or corrupt political activities. Neither of those activities leave room for a democratic and free society. That is why much of our efforts in Bosnia were directed to fighting organized crime and political corruption.

What concerns me now is that I fear that we are losing that economic and social mobility in our society. I am well aware that in this audience tonight are many people who have been unusually successful in changing their circumstances in life through hard-work, creativity and willingness to take risks. I acknowledge that it can still be done.

However, the overwhelming data indicate that fewer people are able to make that transition and that this unfavorable trend is accelerating. The data lead to the conclusion that it is becoming increasingly less likely that someone born in poverty will make that transition and it is becoming increasingly more likely that someone born to less-educated and less-affluent parents will be unsuccessful in changing their economic and social status through the institutions that have historically enabled such a transition.

There are many factors that explain why that change has occurred and why it is less likely that people will be successful in making that transition. A lot of politicians tell you that there are simple explanations for that trend. They will tell you that it is the result of unfair tax policies or trade policies or conscious public policy choices which have caused those results. They will tell you that they have definitive solutions to cure the problem. They will say that all you have to do is tax the super-rich more or erect trade barriers or implement vast new social programs and the problem will be cured.

Unfortunately, I think the problem is much more complex and that no one-sentence answer will restore the opportunities which our society needs to offer. Some of the answers are political but others are cultural. I cannot pretend to offer answers but can urge that we have a discussion to address the issue. I believe that our success in restoring the opportunities for upward mobility will largely determine what kind of society my generation will leave for our children and grandchildren.

The problem has many causes including technological changes which have eliminated unskilled manufacturing jobs, cultural changes which have destabilized traditional families, deficiencies in our educational system which leave young people unprepared to work in a knowledge-based economy.

Someone described the modern factory workforce as a man and a dog: the man is there to feed the dog and the dog is there to insure that the man does not touch the machinery. I am not suggesting that technological change is bad. Technological changes have brought enormous benefits to society. But I am suggesting that we can do a better job of adapting to these changes by understanding and considering the effects that these changes will cause. It is particularly essential that we foresee these effects in order to prepare a workforce with skills that are relevant to the economy resulting from those changes.

We spend enormous resources in educating our children. Our per-capita expenditures far exceed the expenditures of the countries which have been most successful in preparing their students. The data indicate to me that those early years of development are critical and that a child born into poverty will probably enter kindergarten with a deficit that the system will never be able to overcome. A child who reaches public school without nurturing, without having been exposed to reading, without having learned the enjoyment of learning begins with a disadvantage that it is unlikely will be overcome no matter how much money we pour into K through 12 education. We need to find programs which successfully teach essential parenting skills, and which teach preschoolers to enjoy learning, with particular emphasis on reading. If this sounds like a sinister program of government paternalism that we cannot afford, consider that the alternatives are even bigger and more expensive government programs like welfare, criminal justice, unemployment, and incarceration.

Perhaps no factor has impacted upward mobility more than the disintegration of the traditional two-parent family. I raise this not as a moral or a religious issue. It is a socio-economic issue. The evidence is incontrovertible that the single most important factor in predicting whether a child will succeed in school, avoid criminal conduct, gain meaningful employment and become a contributing member of society is being raised and nurtured by two parents. But, yet, our society seems to continue to undervalue the importance of two-parent families and has almost tacitly endorsed the idea of giving birth without marriage. I suggest that the reversal of this trend is an essential part of restoring the upward mobility so essential to the free-market economy.

Another factor which has greatly inhibited the upward mobility which we value has been the epidemic of drug addiction and substance abuse. It is not an issue at the forefront of public discourse these days. We have, it seems to me, almost become inured to its pervasiveness so we would rather not discuss it. During my entire lifetime, we have tried to deal with this issue through the criminal justice system. We have spent tens of billions of dollars within the criminal justice system and have seriously compromised the system in doing so. And we have utterly and completely failed to reduce the problem. Perhaps it is time to deal with substance abuse and addiction as a public health crisis rather than a criminal justice issue. We have experienced a lot of success in addressing public health issues. It is time to try a different approach.

I have mentioned only a few of the factors which obviously inhibit upward mobility within our economic system. I am sure that there are many others which we could discuss. One's political leanings will largely influence the manner in which they view the causes and the solutions for this problem. What cannot be debated, however, it seems to me, is that upward mobility is an essential part of a free economy and that the decline in the frequency of upward mobility threatens our free-market system and, by threatening that system, threatens the free society which is the very foundation of western civilization.

Thanks for your indulgence in allowing a senior citizen to vent and thanks for this recognition.

Acknowledgments

My experiences in Bosnia and Herzegovina were priceless. I developed too many friendships to mention them all, so I will mention only a few of them. It was a rare privilege to work with Lord Paddy Ashdown. He is perhaps the most charismatic leader I have known and I cherish the friendship I developed with him. His premature death was a great loss for Great Britain. Ambassador Don Hays became a great friend, too. He is a remarkably empathetic person beneath a gruff exterior. My friend Chip Erdmann, who served as a judge of the Montana Supreme Court and, later, as a judge of the U.S. Court of Appeals for the Armed Forces, not only recruited me to the Office of the High Representative but provided the plan for legal reform which I was charged to implement.

Thanks to the administrators and faculty of Holy Trinity Episcopal Academy, who invited me to speak to their 2010 graduates. My friend Cathy Ford was then the head of the school and founded the Upper School, creating remarkable learning opportunities for students. My grandchildren benefited greatly from those opportunities.

My afternoon with Ted Williams occurred only because of my friendship with Andy Seminick. I miss Andy very much. Andy was a fierce competitor on the baseball diamond, but he was also a gentle, compassionate, and generous man off the field.

My son-in-law Scott Bell invited me to join him on the Atlantic crossing. I, in turn, told my Montana friend Bob Lindeke about the opportunity to join the crew, an offer he readily accepted. We enjoyed a compatible crew with Scott, Bob, Dave Underhill, and Bob Snyder. Since Bob Lindeke and I were by far the oldest crew members and I was by far the least competent sailor, I greatly appreciate the patience and kindness of my fellow crew members.

The Space Coast Business Hall of Fame is part of Junior Achievement of the Space Coast. Its dynamic leader is Anne Conroy-Baiter, whose energy and creativity have transformed it into an extraordinarily effective community asset.

This is the third book for which Lois Deveneau has done the formatting and cover design and guided me to self-publish. I appreciate that I have not exhausted her patience and that she continues to assist me so effectively. I feel that we have developed a friendship along the way.

Finally, as with all of the books I have written, I appreciate the fact that my wife Wendy tolerates it when I retreat to my office which is littered with news articles and publications while I isolate myself to write. Moreover, she has tolerated and facilitated the experiences related to this book, even sometimes participating in the adventures as exhibited by her willingness to uproot our home and relocate to Sarajevo. I should add thanks to my children, Alison, Andy, and Carrie, who also unhesitatingly facilitated that adventure.

Bibliography

Bradlee, Ben, Jr.:
"The Kid, The Immortal Life of Ted Williams." Little, Brown and Company 2013.

Halberstam, David:
"Everything They Had: Sports Writing from David Halberstam." Hyperion 2008.

Potter, William:
"A Bosnian Diary: A Floridian's Experiences in Nation-Building." Florida Historical Society 2005.

Roberts, Robin and Rogers, C. Paul, III:
"The Whiz Kids and the 1950 Pennant." Temple University Press 1996.

Russell, Jane:
"The Atlantic Crossing Guide, 7th Edition." RCC Pilotage Foundation 2018.

About the Author

William C. Potter is a graduate of Brown University and the University of Michigan Law School. He practiced law in Florida from 1965 until 2002, serving as president of the firm of Potter, McClelland, Marks, and Healy and, later, as a partner in the firm of Holland & Knight. Potter is a retired officer of the Florida Air National Guard, where he served as Judge Advocate General for Florida.

In 2002, he moved to Europe to Head the Rule of Law Department of the Office of the High Representative (OHR) in Bosnia and Herzegovina. OHR was responsible for administering the Dayton Peace Agreement, which ended the brutal war in the Balkans during the early 1990s.

He served as a director of what is now the Melbourne Regional Chamber for more than 25 years, serving as chair in 1974 and 1984. He also served on the boards of several banks and businesses, including a publicly traded defense contractor and an insurance company.

He served as legal counsel for the Melbourne Airport Authority for over 25 years and has been a member for 18 years. He is currently the authority's chair.

He served as a Trustee of the Florida Institute of Technology from 1980 to 2022, including serving as Chair from 1990 to 1997. He currently serves as Trustee Emeritus.

He was inducted into the Florida Tech Sports Hall of Fame in 2017 and the Space Coast Business Hall of Fame in 2016.

He is the author of *A Bosnian Diary: A Floridian's Experience in Nation-Building*, published by the Florida Historical Society in 2005, and *Melbourne Orlando International Airport: A History from 1928 to 2022*, self-published in 2022. Potter also co-authored *A History of Intercollegiate Athletics at Florida Institute of Technology: 1958 to 2023*, published in 2023.

He and his wife, Wendy, are the parents of 3 children and grandparents of 3 grandchildren. They divide their time between Indialantic, Florida, and Red Lodge, Montana.

www.ingramcontent.com/pod-product-compliance
Lightning Source LLC
LaVergne TN
LVHW070446070526
838199LV00037B/707